HEARING
SOUNDS

© Aladdin Books Ltd 1994
Created and produced by
NW Books, 28 Percy Street
London W1P OLD

*First published in the United States in 1995
by Copper Beech Books, an imprint of
The Millbrook Press, 2 Old New Milford Road
Brookfield, Connecticut 06804*

Editor:
Susannah Le Besque

Design:
David West Children's Book Design
Illustrator:
Tony Kenyon
Photography:
Roger Vlitos
Consultant:
Dr. Bryson Gore

The publishers wish to point out
that all the photographs reproduced
in this book have been posed by models.

Library of Congress Cataloging-in-Publication Data
Gibson,. Gary, 1957-
Hearing Sounds / by Gary Gibson : illustrated by
Tony Kenyon. p. cm. -- (Science for fun)
Includes index.
ISBN 1-56294-614-5 (lib. bdg.)
ISBN 1-56294-632-3 (pbk.)
1. Sound--Juvenile literature. 2. Sound--
Experiments--Juvenile literature. 3. Sounds--
Experiments--Juvenile literature. [1. Sound--
Experiments. 2. Experiments.] I. Kenyon, Tony,
ill. II. Title. III. Series: Gibson, Gary, 1957-
Science for fun.
QC225.5.G53   1995   94-41187
534'.078--dc20   CIP AC

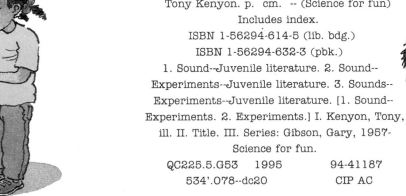

SCIENCE FOR FUN

HEARING SOUNDS

GARY GIBSON

COPPER BEECH BOOKS
Brookfield, Connecticut

CONTENTS

INTRODUCTION

Sounds are all around us in the air. Sounds warn us of danger, and bring us the pleasure of music. But *how* do musical instruments make sounds? How does a telephone work? Scientists have found out a lot about how sound is created and how it travels. This book

contains a selection of exciting "hands-on" projects to help explain some of the fascinating discoveries that have been made about sound.

GET AN ADULT TO DO THIS FOR YOU

Whenever this symbol appears adult supervision is required.

WHAT IS A SOUND?

All sounds are made by something moving. Gently rest your fingertips on your throat as you talk. You can feel your throat vibrating. Vocal cords in your throat move as you speak and make the air in your throat and mouth vibrate. The vibrating air makes sounds.

MAKE A BANGER

1 Take a square sheet of paper and decorate it. Fold it in half diagonally to make a triangle (see right).

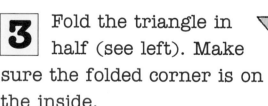
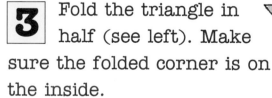

Fold

2 Fold the top right-hand corner downward.

Flap

3 Fold the triangle in half (see left). Make sure the folded corner is on the inside.

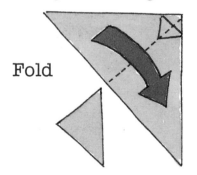

Fold

4 Make a crease down the middle but do not fold in half.

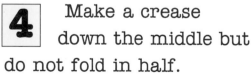

Crease

Fold

5 From the open end of the triangle fold the top layer of paper over along the crease. Flip the triangle over and repeat.

6 Grasp the three pointed ends of the triangle together. Flick your wrist down to make the banger work.

WHY IT WORKS

Flicking your wrist makes the folded paper jump out of place. The paper pushes hard against the air. The pushed air reaches your ears as a "bang."

Air

FURTHER IDEAS

Try making different sized bangers. Follow the same steps with the largest square of paper you can find. Repeat with the smallest square of paper.

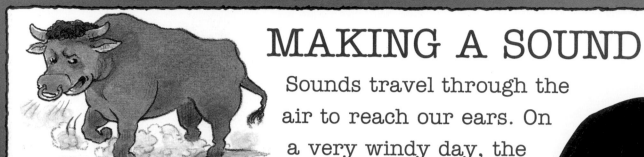

MAKING A SOUND

Sounds travel through the air to reach our ears. On a very windy day, the wind can blow sounds away from you so it is difficult to hear a conversation. If sounds have traveled a long way then they lose some loudness. Sounds made close to us seem louder.

MAKE A BULL ROARER

1 You will need a long cardboard tube, scissors, a ruler, about 19 inches of clothing elastic and three to six feet of string.

2 Loop the elastic through the tube. Knot the two ends together firmly.

3 Knot one end of the string around the elastic at the opening of the tube.

4 Take the other end of the string in your hand and swing the bull roarer around. Listen to the sound it makes.

WHY IT WORKS

As the tube spins around, air enters and pushes the elastic rapidly backward and forward. Air leaving the tube carries the sounds made from these movements.

Air carrying sound out

Air in

FURTHER IDEAS
Experiment with the bull roarer by using a shorter length of string. If you have room, try a longer length. Listen carefully. How does the difference in length affect the sound?

GOOD VIBRATIONS

Pleasant sounds can come from musical instruments. All musical instruments have parts that move to make vibrations. Vibrations are caused by something moving back and forth very quickly and smoothly. A drum has a skin that vibrates when it is hit with a stick. The harder you hit the drum, the bigger the vibrations and the louder the sound.

MAKE A DRUM

1 You will need a large, empty tin can and a clean plastic bag. Carefully cut a circle out of the plastic bag. Make sure it is larger than the can.

2 Stretch the circle of plastic as tightly as you can over the rim of the empty can. Hold it in place with tape.

3 Cut a strip of paper the same width as the can and long enough to go all the way around it. Color it brightly and tape into place.

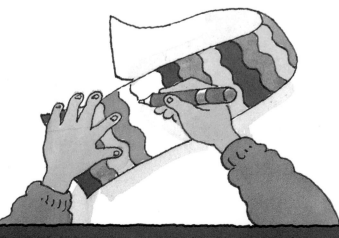

4 Make a pair of drumsticks with wooden dowels. Wrap the tips in cotton and cover with a piece of stocking. Tie into place with string.

5 Test your drum. Hit the drumskin gently in different places and compare the sounds of different vibrations. Try to play a rhythm.

WHY IT WORKS

When you hit the drumskin it vibrates. The air inside the drum vibrates too. These vibrations of air are called sound waves.

FURTHER IDEAS
The movement of the vibrating drumskin is too small to see. Try placing some dried peas on the drum to show the effect of the vibrations.

THE SOUND DRUM

We cannot see sounds but we can see their effects. Sounds travel through the air just like waves in the sea. If the waves are strong enough they can move things in their path. The human ear has an eardrum that moves when hit by sound waves entering the ear.

MAKE A SOUND DRUM

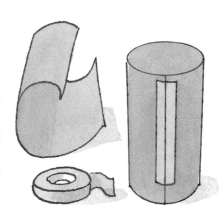

1 Roll a strong sheet of cardboard into a tube. Make sure the cardboard overlaps so that it can be taped together.

2 Cut a circle larger than the end of your tube out of a clean plastic bag. Tape it as tightly as possible over one end of the tube.

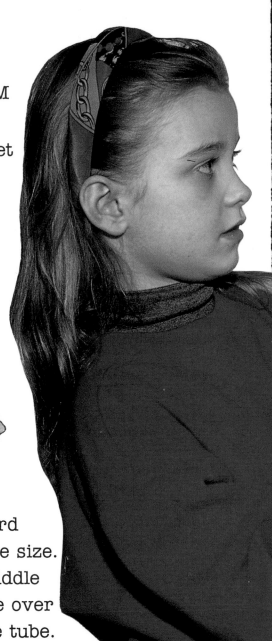

3 Cut a cardboard circle the same size. Cut a hole in the middle of it. Tape the circle over the other end of the tube.

4 Make a target out of a long strip of tissue paper. Cut one end into a long fringe.

5 Point the hole in the bottom of your sound drum toward your target. Tap the plastic drumskin. What happens to your target?

WHY IT WORKS

Tapping the drumskin pushes sound waves through the hole in the bottom of the drum. It also forces rings of air out through the hole, which moves the paper fringe.

FURTHER IDEAS
You need a partner to help you. Take turns to hit the sound drum and hold the target. What is the farthest distance you can hit the target from?

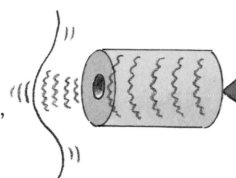

LISTEN CLOSELY

If you are ill a doctor may use a stethoscope to listen to your heart or lungs. You may have a problem breathing or your heart may not be making the sounds it is supposed to. These sounds are normally too quiet to hear. A stethoscope magnifies them so they can be heard.

MAKE A STETHOSCOPE

1 Cut out two large paper circles. Color them brightly. Make a long cardboard tube. Decorate this too.

2 Cut a hole in the center of each circle the same size as the tube end. Cut from the hole to the edge of the circle. Tape the edges to form two cones.

3 Tape one cone shape over each end of the tube. Make the fit as snug as possible.

sound in

4 Now try out your stethoscope. Put your ear to one cone and place the other on a friend's chest.

WHY IT WORKS

As sound waves spread out they become smaller and harder to hear. The first cone stops them from spreading by collecting them together. They move along the tube and out through the second cone into your ear.

FURTHER IDEAS
Use your stethoscope to compare the sound of your heartbeat with your friend's heartbeat. Try to think of other quiet sounds to listen to, such as a friend whispering or a ticking watch.

BOUNCING SOUNDS

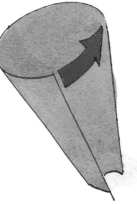

Bats have very poor eyesight yet can fly around safely in complete darkness. They can avoid hitting obstacles by bouncing squeaky sounds off them. Bouncing sounds are called echoes. You can hear echoes in places such as large halls or gyms when sounds bounce off the walls.

BOUNCE AN ECHO

2 One cone is a hearing aid, the other a megaphone to magnify sounds.

1 Cut the shape shown here out of cardboard. Overlap the edges and tape to make a cone. Repeat so you have two large cones.

Cut out two strips of cardboard. Tape them along the sides of your hearing aid and megaphone to make handles.

WHY IT WORKS

When a sound wave hits something it can either be absorbed or bounce off. Smooth, flat surfaces bounce sounds best. The sound of your voice bounces off the mirror just as light would.

Hearing aid

Megaphone

FURTHER IDEAS

Try to bounce sounds off other surfaces. You could compare a cork tile, an egg carton and a wooden block. Which reflects sound waves best?

4 Talk into the megaphone aimed at a mirror or tin tray. A friend can hear your voice echo with the hearing aid.

KEEPING SOUNDS IN

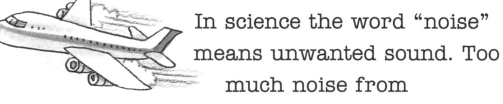

In science the word "noise" means unwanted sound. Too much noise from airplanes or discos is bad for your health. It can keep you from sleeping and even damage your eardrums. A radio studio is soundproofed. Noise is kept out so that it cannot be heard when programs are broadcast.

MAKE A SOUNDPROOF BOX

1 You need a large cardboard box and a shoe box, both with lids. The shoe box must easily fit inside the cardboard box.

2 Decorate the outside of the cardboard box. Use brightly colored paints. When dry, place the shoe box inside the larger box.

3 Pack the space between the boxes with crumpled newspapers. Add a little paper to the inner box.

WHY IT WORKS

Sound waves from the alarm cannot escape from the soundproof box. Most sound waves are absorbed by the cardboard and the newspaper. You may hear just a few sound waves leaking out.

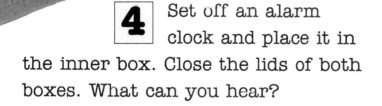

4 Set off an alarm clock and place it in the inner box. Close the lids of both boxes. What can you hear?

FURTHER IDEAS
Try to improve the soundproofing by replacing the newspaper with egg cartons or sawdust. Make it a fair test by using the same alarm clock each time.

VIBRATING AIR

An orchestra has percussion, wind, and stringed instruments. Wind instruments include flutes, clarinets, and recorders. They are all made out of a tube. When the instrument is played, air inside the tube vibrates and makes sound. Instruments make different sounds because they vary in shape and size.

MAKE A CLARINET

1 Use stiff cardboard to make a cone as shown on page 16. Make sure the small opening at the top is less than half an inch across.

2 Use sharp scissors to cut a "V" shape from the end of a drinking straw.

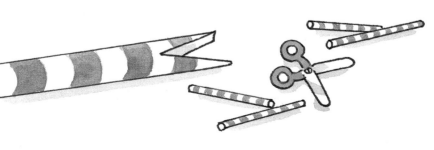

3 Hold the cut end of the straw between your thumb and finger. Pinch the ends together to flatten them.

4 Cut off the pinched end of the straw. Push it into the small opening of the cone.

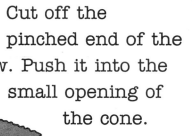

Sound out

5 Try out your clarinet. Put the mouthpiece inside your mouth and blow into the cone. Feel it vibrate as you play a note.

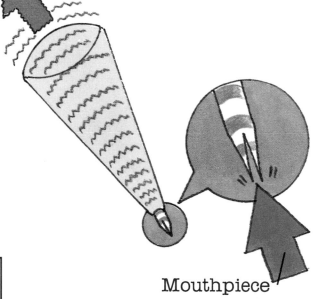

Mouthpiece

FURTHER IDEAS
Make more clarinets using cones of different sizes. Each needs a straw mouthpiece as before. Compare the kinds of notes you get with long and short clarinets. Using your different-sized clarinets can you and your friends play a tune?

WHY IT WORKS

Blowing through the sharp edges of the straw makes them vibrate. The vibrating straw makes all the air in the cone vibrate and causes sound. We hear these sound waves escaping from the cone.

DIFFERENT PITCHES

Most musical instruments can make a wide range of notes – from low or deep notes that you may be able to feel, to high notes you can only just hear.

Notes differ in pitch. Pitch measures how high or low a note is.

MAKE A XYLOPHONE

GET AN ADULT TO DO THIS FOR YOU

1 Cut five circles in the lid of a box, big enough for glass bottles to fit.

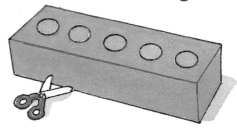

2 Check that the bottles fit snugly into place. Tape a sheet of cardboard to stand up behind them.

3 Fill each bottle with a different amount of water. Line them up with the fullest at one end and the emptiest at the other.

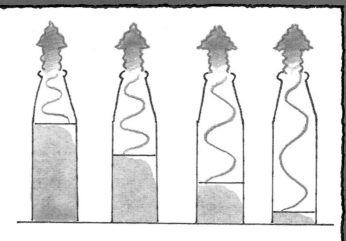

WHY IT WORKS

Above the water level each bottle contains a tube of air. Hitting the bottles makes the air vibrate. Longer tubes of air (emptier bottles) vibrate more slowly. Slower vibrations make deeper (lower pitched) sounds.

4 Tap the neck of each bottle with a stick or wooden spoon. Note the different sounds they make. See if you can play a tune.

FURTHER IDEAS
You can make the air in the bottles vibrate another way. Rest your lip on the bottle top and blow.

VIBRATING STRINGS

Stringed instruments include violins, harps and guitars. Musicians hit or pluck the strings to make them vibrate. Each string is of a different thickness and tautness so each makes a different note. Musicians also change the notes by altering the length of the vibrating string.

MAKE A GUITAR

1 Wash out a large margarine tub. Cut an oval-shaped hole in the lid with a sharp knife or pair of scissors.

GET AN ADULT TO DO THIS FOR YOU

2 Use brightly colored magic markers to decorate the outside of the tub and lid.

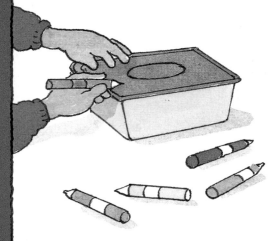

3 Wrap six rubber bands of differing thickness lengthwise around the tub. Leave a space between each rubber band.

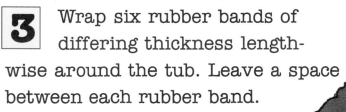

4 Pluck each rubber band with your finger. Compare the sounds made by plucking the ends or middle of each rubber band.

Slower vibrations - lower notes

Faster vibrations - higher notes

WHY IT WORKS

A vibrating rubber band makes the air in the tub vibrate. This makes sound waves which escape through the hole in the lid. Thin rubber bands vibrate much faster than thicker ones. Faster vibrations make higher notes.

FURTHER IDEAS
Place a pencil between the rubber bands and the lid of the tub. This alters the length of the rubber bands and changes the notes they make. Experiment with the pencil in different places along the tub.

TUNING UP

Musicians have to "tune" their instruments. For a stringed instrument this means adjusting each string to just the right tautness to play the correct note. If a string is too slack, it cannot vibrate properly. If it is too taut then the string might snap.

MAKE A SONOMETER

1 You will need a large sheet of thick cardboard. Divide roughly into thirds. Decorate one side with colored magic markers.

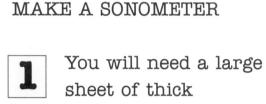

GET AN ADULT TO DO THIS FOR YOU

2 Very carefully use a sharp knife to cut a notch into the sides of two wooden pencils.

3 Find a piece of nylon fishing line about three feet long. Firmly push a thumbtack into one end of the cardboard. Tie one end of the thread to the thumbtack.

4 Tape the notched pencils into place. Lay the fishing line in the two notches. Tie the other end of the line around a plastic cup weighted down with marbles or stones.

5 Hang the cup over the edge of a table. Pluck the fishing line. Listen to the sound change when you add marbles to the cup.

WHY IT WORKS

Hanging more weight from the fishing line pulls it tighter. This causes it to vibrate faster. The faster the vibrations are the higher the note sounds to us.

FURTHER IDEAS
Change the length of fishing line you pluck by moving the pencils closer together or farther apart. Try to predict the length of line and weight to attach to get the highest and lowest possible notes.

FAR AWAY SOUNDS

Listening to the ground is an excellent way of listening to far away sounds. This is because sounds travel faster through the ground than through air. You may have seen a bandit in a cowboy film put his ear to a railway track. Today railway workers use this method to listen for trains. They hear sound trapped in the rails before they see the train.

GET AN ADULT TO DO THIS FOR YOU

MAKE A TELEPHONE

1 Find two identical plastic cups. Punch a small hole in the bottom of each with a sharp pencil.

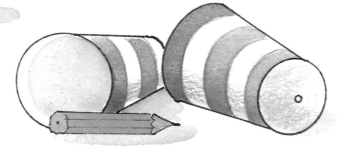

2 Knot one end of a long length of string. Feed the other end through the hole in each cup. Now knot the other end of the string.

3 Check that the string cannot be easily tugged out of place. Decorate each telephone cup. Use brightly colored magic markers.

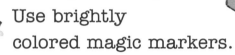

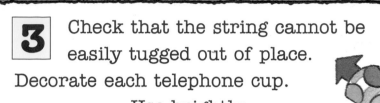

WHY IT WORKS

The sounds you make travel along the string as tiny vibrations (you can just feel them if you touch the string). They travel through the plastic cup and the air to reach your ear.

4 With a partner, each take a cup and pull the string taut. Put your cup to your ear. Ask your partner to talk into theirs. Try to have a conversation.

FURTHER IDEAS
Tie a fork and spoon to a piece of string. Hold the other end of the string to one ear; cover up your other ear. You can "feel" the sound of the jangling utensils. The sounds travel up through the string.

FANTASTIC SOUND FACTS

Sound travels through air at an amazing 1,115 feet per second. However, the hotter the air, the faster sound travels.

The farthest the human voice has traveled without a microphone is 10 miles across still water at night.

The loudest known explosion occurred August 27, 1883 when a volcano called Krakatoa erupted on a tiny island off the coast of Sumatra. The island collapsed into the sea and the explosion was heard an incredible 3,106 miles away.

In 1877 Thomas Edison made the first sound recording using a cylinder covered in tin foil. He called his invention the phonograph – a very early type of record player.

The first person to fly faster than the speed of sound was Captain Charles E. Yeager in a rocket plane called Bell X-1. The Bell X-1 achieved a speed of 698 mph on October 14, 1947.

Sound with frequencies above the range of human hearing are called ultrasound. Ultrasounds can be used to "look" inside the human body. A computer converts the ultrasound echoes into a picture. This method is used to look at unborn babies to ensure they are growing properly.

Some singers have been able to break a glass with the notes they sing. This happens because objects naturally vibrate at a certain rate. If a sound near them is vibrating at the same rate, then the vibrations increase and the glass can shatter.

The telephone was invented in 1876 by the Scottish inventor Alexander Graham Bell. "Mr. Watson, come here, I want you," was the first telephone message sent by Bell to his assistant.

The oldest known musical instruments are 40,000-year-old whistles made from reindeer toe bones.

GLOSSARY

Eardrum
Sheet of skin inside your ear. Sounds in the air set it vibrating just like a drumskin. Messages to the brain tell you what the sound is like.

Echo
The reflection or bouncing back of a sound from a surface.

Frequency
The number of sound vibrations that happen in one second.

Note
A steady sound or tone of the same pitch or frequency.

Pitch
The highness or lowness of a sound. Pitch depends on the frequency of the vibration causing the sound.

Percussion
Musical instruments played by hitting two things together; for example, a drum and drumstick.

Reflect
Bounce back from a surface.

Sound wave
A regular pattern of vibrations that move through the air or other materials.

Stethoscope
Instrument used by doctors to hear sounds within your body normally too quiet to hear.

Vibration
A rapid backward and forward movement.

Vocal cord
Flaps of elastic tissue in the human throat which vibrate as air from the lungs is pushed over them, producing the sounds of the human voice.

Woodwind
Wind instruments made from wood or sometimes silver; for example, a clarinet or a flute.

INDEX